George Washington

George Washington was the first President of the United States. He was a great leader.

George Washington took the oath of office in New York City. He promised to defend the Constitution.

Coins to remember the special day

Before he became President, George did many things.

He was a land surveyor.

He was a colonel in the Virginia Militia.

George Washington loved music. This artist has shown him playing the flute.

3

George Washington was the general and leader of the United States Army.

This famous painting shows General Washington and his soldiers crossing the Delaware River.

Leading his soldiers

This was a special merit badge George Washington gave to soldiers.

5

George Washington led many battles against Great Britain.

Often George Washington's troops went hungry and barefoot in the snow.

Helping a soldier

Each star on this flag from long ago stands for one of the original 13 colonies.

He helped the United States win its freedom from Great Britain.

At the Constitutional Convention in Philadelphia

7

George Washington was a great leader.
He is called the Father of His Country.

Let's Explore!

This map shows Mount Vernon, Virginia, where George Washington lived. Read the key. Find out what each number means.

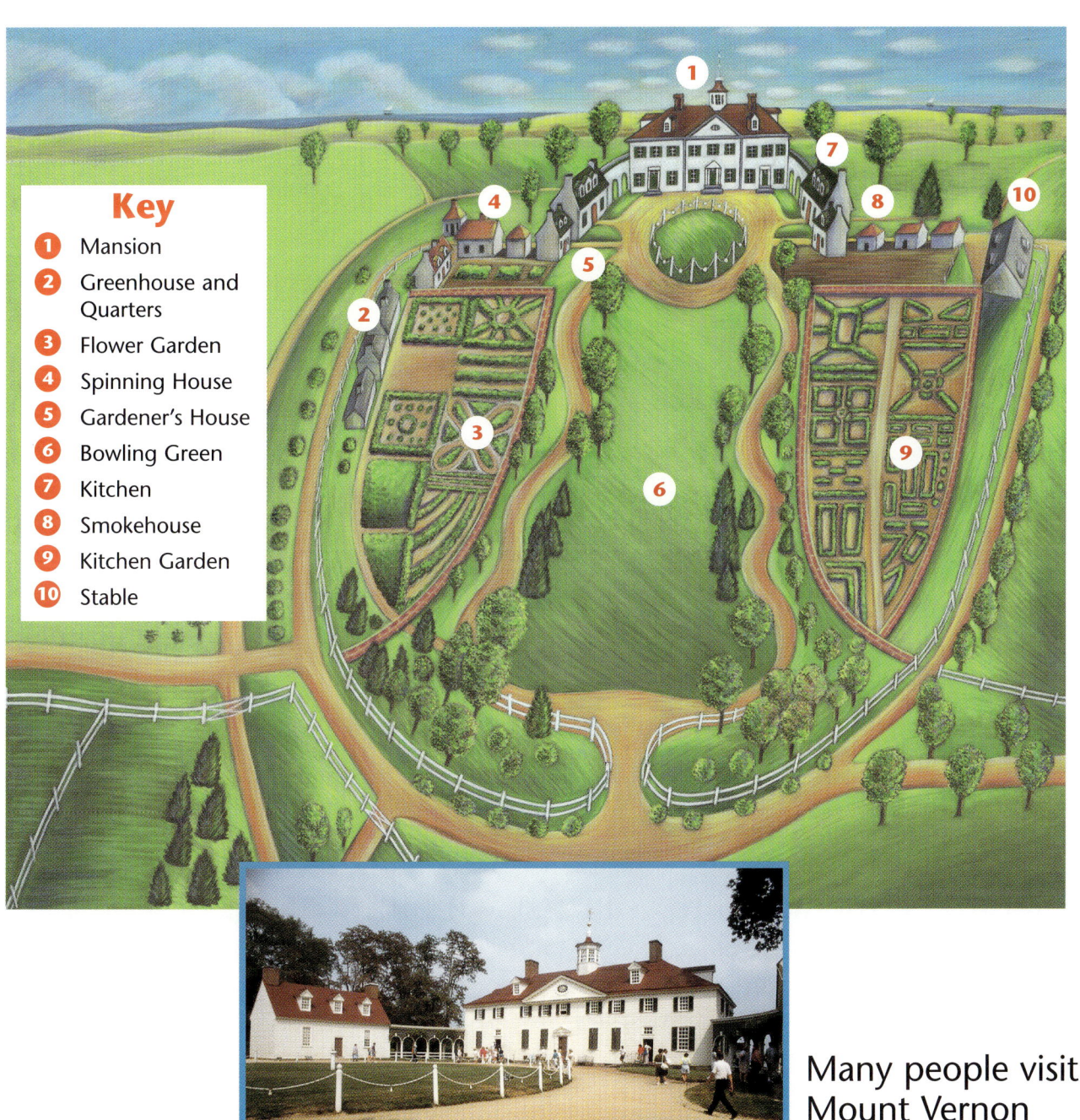

Key
1. Mansion
2. Greenhouse and Quarters
3. Flower Garden
4. Spinning House
5. Gardener's House
6. Bowling Green
7. Kitchen
8. Smokehouse
9. Kitchen Garden
10. Stable

Many people visit Mount Vernon each year.

What Do You Think?

George Washington Stamp

Washington's face appears on many things such as stamps and coins. Create a stamp honoring George Washington. You could show him as a grown-up or as a child. Tell about your stamp and how much it costs.

The Washington Monument

The monument is slightly over 555 feet high and took longer than 36 years to build. Use clay or paper to make your own model of the Washington Monument. Tell about the monument and what shape it is.

George's Name

Many places and things are named for George Washington. See how many things you can list that have George's name or his picture on them. Share your list with the class. Then see how many words you can make out of the 16 letters in his name.

WASHINGTON

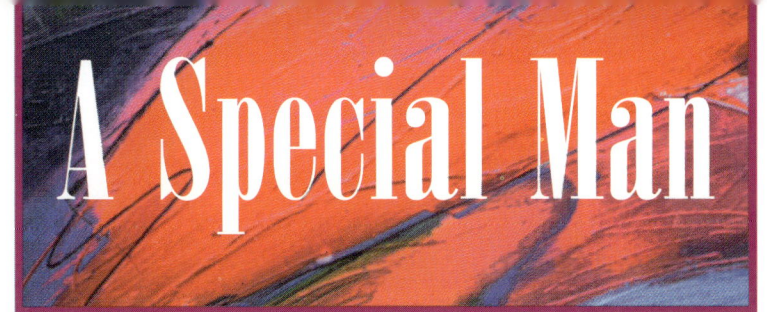
A Special Man

George Washington was liked and respected. He was the subject of many artists' works.

by Currier and Ives

by George Hicks

by Gilbert Stuart

by John Trumbull

More About George Washington

George Washington was born in Virginia in 1732. He died in 1799.

He was over six feet tall, which was tall for his time.

As a young man, he was a land surveyor.

He married Martha Custis. She was a widow with two children.

He had sets of false teeth made from wood, from ivory, and even from hippopotamus tusk.

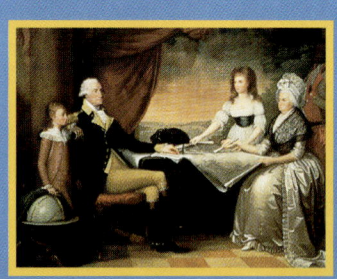

It's been said that one of his favorite foods was ice cream.

He loved his home, Mount Vernon, Virginia.